Date: 9/24/15

J BIO GANDHI
Diemer, Lauren,
Gandhi /

D1088578

History Makers

Gandhi

by Lauren Diemer

www.av2books.com

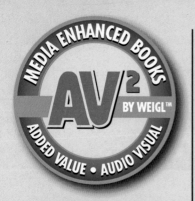

AV² provides enriched content that supplements and complements this book. Weigl's AV² books strive to create inspired learning and engage young minds in a total learning experience.

Your AV² Media Enhanced books come alive with...

Audio
Listen to sections of the book read aloud.

Key Words
Study vocabulary, and complete a matching word activity.

Video
Watch informative video clips.

Quizzes
Test your knowledge.

Embedded Weblinks
Gain additional information for research.

Slide Show
View images and captions, and prepare a presentation.

Try This!
Complete activities and hands-on experiments.

... and much, much more!

Go to **www.av2books.com**, and enter this book's unique code.

BOOK CODE

J695239

AV² by Weigl brings you media enhanced books that support active learning.

Published by AV² by Weigl
350 5th Avenue, 59th Floor
New York, NY 10118

www.av2books.com   www.weigl.com

Library of Congress Control Number: 2013953121

ISBN 978-1-4896-0624-2 (hardcover)
ISBN 978-1-4896-0625-9 (softcover)
ISBN 978-1-4896-0626-6 (Single user eBook)
ISBN 978-1-4896-0627-3 (Multi-user eBook)

Printed in the United States of America in North Mankato, Minnesota
1 2 3 4 5 6 7 8 9 0 17 16 15 14 13

WEP301113
122013

Editor: Megan Cuthbert
Design: Tammy West

Photograph Credits
Weigl acknowledges Getty Images as the primary image supplier for this title. Every reasonable effort has been made to trace ownership and to obtain permission to reprint copyright material. The publishers would be pleased to have any errors or omissions brought to their attention so that they may be corrected in subsequent printings.

Contents

"The force of love by peace always wins over violence."

Who Was Mohandas Gandhi?

Mohandas Gandhi was a civil rights activist. Among his many achievements, he helped India gain independence from Great Britain. Gandhi has been called the "father of India." He was also known as Mahatma, "the great-souled one." Gandhi had many followers and supporters all over the world, especially in India. He worked for fairness and **equality** for the Indian people.

Gandhi believed the best way to bring about change for his people was through **non-violent** means. He would stage hunger strikes as a form of non-violent protest. Gandhi believed a person should not bring harm to any other living being or have many material things. He tried to live by these principles and lead by example.

Growing Up

Mohandas Karamchand Gandhi was born on October 2, 1869, in Porbandar, India. Gandhi's father, Karamchand Gandhi, was the *dewan*, or chief minister, of Porbandar. A dewan was a high-ranking politician in India. Gandhi's father did not have much education, but he was a successful politician.

Gandhi's mother, Putlibai, was a very religious woman. She followed the **Hindu** religion. Hindus believe that all life is sacred. This was one reason why Putlibai was a vegetarian. She also believed that everyone should respect one another, regardless of religion.

Growing up, Gandhi was quite shy. His shyness made it difficult for him to make friends in school. He was also afraid of many things, including the dark. At 13 years old, Gandhi was married to Kasturbai Makanji. It was common for Indian parents to choose a husband or wife for their children.

◀ **Gandhi was very close to his eldest brother, Laxmidas.**

Get to Know India

IRAN   AFGHANISTAN

PAKISTAN

CHINA

NEPAL

INDIA

BURMA

SCALE

N

0   500 Miles

0   500 Kilometers

India has the fastest growing population in the world. Its population is currently more than 1.1 billion people. China is the only country with a higher population.

The largest city in India is Mumbai. Bollywood, India's film industry, is located in Mumbai.

NATIONAL SYMBOLS

TREE
Banyan Tree

The capital of India is New Delhi.

BIRD
Indian Peacock

FLOWER
Lotus

The Taj Mahal in Agra, India, took about 20 years to build. The popular tourist attraction draws millions of visitors every year.

Practice Makes Perfect

Gandhi went to university in India in 1887. He found school very difficult because all of his classes were in English. Gandhi decided to go to school in England to become a lawyer. As a lawyer, he could follow in his father's footsteps. In England, Gandhi tried to fit in by adopting the English lifestyle. He wore fancy clothes and took dance lessons, but it did not feel right. He decided to go back to the simple way of life he grew up with in India.

After completing his law degree, Gandhi went home to India. On his return, he had a difficult time. Gandhi learned that his mother had died while he was away. He also was unable to find a job at first. Being shy, he had trouble practicing law. Finally, in 1893, Gandhi accepted a job in South Africa, working on a legal case.

◀ In 1903, Gandhi moved to the South African city of Johannesburg, where he set up his own law firm.

South Africa, like India, was under British rule. Many Indians moved to South Africa to work in mines or on farms. Indians had very few rights in South Africa. They could not vote or own land. When Gandhi wore his traditional turban into a South African courtroom, he was told to remove it. Indians were not allowed to wear hats around white people. He refused and walked out of the courtroom.

Gandhi vowed to get rid of **prejudice** against the Indian people in South Africa. However, he would not use violence to accomplish it. Gandhi's shyness began to disappear. His new sense of purpose gave him strength.

QUICK FACTS

- Gandhi was a vegetarian. He did not believe in harming living things.
- Gandhi's birthday is a national holiday in India.
- Gandhi spoke English with an Irish accent because one of his teachers was Irish.

◀ Gandhi wore a turban because it was part of Indian cultural dress. He continued to wear his turban in South Africa as an act of defiance against South African laws.

Key Events

In 1907, the government in the Transvaal region of South Africa passed a law called the Black Act. Under the law, black and Indian people were not given the same rights as white South Africans. Gandhi refused to cooperate with the government and obey the law. On November 6, 1913, he led a non-violent protest. More than 2,200 Indian people joined him. Gandhi was arrested for leading the resistance. More people went on strike in support of Gandhi's protest. Soon, 50,000 people were on strike. The government knew it could not put that many people in jail. In June 1914, the Black Act was repealed. Gandhi's protest had been successful.

Gandhi returned to India in 1915. He felt he had done all he could for the Indians in South Africa. Indians in his homeland needed someone to help lead them to independence from Great Britain. Gandhi also wanted equality for India's poor.

Four years after Gandhi's return to India, the British government passed an act in an attempt to stop political unrest. The act permitted Indians to be arrested and held without a trial. It also allowed people to be tried without a jury. In protest of the act, Gandhi led a *hartal*, a nationwide strike.

▲ Gandhi attended a series of farewell meetings before leaving South Africa forever.

Thoughts from Gandhi

Mohandas Gandhi strived for equality and freedom in his home country of India. He believed in achieving change through non-violent means.

Gandhi talks about how to achieve happiness.
"Happiness is when what you think, what you say, and what you do are in harmony."

Gandhi believes in helping others.
"The best way to find yourself is to lose yourself in the service of others."

Gandhi views non-violence as a way of overcoming differences.
"Belief in non-violence is based on the assumption that human nature in its essence is one and therefore unfailingly responds to the advances of love..."

Gandhi defines bravery.
"In the composition of the truly brave there should be no malice, no anger, no distrust, no fear of death or physical hurt."

Gandhi talks about what makes a person strong.
"Strength does not come from physical capacity. It comes from an indomitable will."

Gandhi believes in the power of action over inaction.
"You may never know what results come of your action, but if you do nothing there will be no result."

What Is a Civil Rights Activist?

Throughout history, groups of people all over the world have been treated unfairly. Civil rights activists, like Gandhi, work to defend the rights of these people. They work to make laws equal for everyone. A civil rights activist attempts to convince local political leaders to change the laws.

Civil rights leaders are often skilled speakers who are able to motivate and inspire people through speeches and arguments. They may organize protests, marches, and **boycotts** to raise awareness about a cause. These protests are meant to put pressure on governments and organizations to change laws.

▲ A statue of Gandhi is part of the Martin Luther King Jr. Memorial in Atlanta, Georgia.

Civil rights activists sometimes become the focus of anger and frustration. They are often threatened and physically harmed. Some are arrested and spend years in jail. Civil rights activists can also be in danger of assassination.

SATYAGRAHA

Satyagraha was a term Gandhi used to describe his form of protest. It means "insistence on truth" in Hindi. Gandhi introduced satyagraha as a form of non-violent protest. It involved non-violent methods, such as not cooperating with the **authorities** when a law is unfair. However, satyagraha stressed the importance of being polite and kind. Gandhi believed that, rather than creating change by overwhelming their opponents, people could change their opponents' beliefs through kindness and understanding.

Activists 101

Martin Luther King, Jr. (1929–1968)

Martin Luther King, Jr. was a pastor for the Baptist church. He fought to end the **segregation** of African American people in the United States. Martin led several non-violent protests and boycotts in an attempt to change unfair laws. He won the Nobel Peace Prize in 1964, when he was 35. Martin Luther King, Jr. was assassinated on April 4, 1968.

Nelson Mandela (1918–2013)

Nelson Mandela was an anti-**apartheid** activist in South Africa. He was imprisoned for 27 years for his part in organizing protests against apartheid. Apartheid ended in South Africa in 1991. In 1993, Nelson Mandela was awarded the Nobel Peace Prize for his work. He became the country's first black president in 1994.

Aung San Suu Kyi (1945–)

Aung San Suu Kyi is a civil rights activist and politician in Burma, also known as Myanmar. She was inspired by Gandhi and led her followers in non-violent protests against the military-run government in Burma. Aung San spent more than 15 years under house arrest because of her activism. She was awarded the Nobel Peace Prize in 1991. In 2012, Aung San was elected to a seat in Burma's parliament.

Malala Yousafzai (1997–)

Malala Yousafzai is a civil rights activist who fights for the education of women. Malala was born in Mingora, Pakistan, in an area controlled by the Taliban. The Taliban banned girls from attending school. Malala spoke out against the Taliban's restrictions on women's education. In 2012, a Taliban gunman shot Malala. She recovered from the attack, and she continues to fight for women's education. In 2013, Malala was nominated for the Nobel Peace Prize.

Influences

Gandhi's mother and her beliefs influenced Gandhi's politics. Putlibai believed that people from all religions should tolerate one another. Gandhi worked very hard for this in his political career. He read books from many religions. He was very influenced by the *Bhagavad Gita*, which contains some of the teachings of Lord Krishna, a Hindu god. Gandhi also read the Koran, an important text about **Islam**, and the Bible, which teaches about **Christianity**.

The writing and ideas of Russian writer Leo Tolstoy were great influences in Gandhi's life. While Tolstoy was Christian, Gandhi grew up believing in Hinduism and **Jainism**. Despite their religious differences, they were good friends and wrote each other regularly.

◀ Leo Tolstoy developed a friendship with Gandhi late in his life. Tolstoy believed in non-violent resistance and was also a vegetarian, like Gandhi.

In John Ruskin's book *Unto This Last,* Ruskin said wealth was a cause for slavery. He describes manual labor as the only way to live. John Ruskin's book was inspiring for Gandhi, especially when Gandhi was setting up his first **ashram**. Gandhi's ashram followed the principle of using manual labor and literacy as a way of finding purpose in life.

THE GANDHI FAMILY

Mohandas was engaged to Kasturbai at the age of seven. The two were married in 1882. The couple had four sons. Harilal was born in 1887, shortly before Gandhi left for England. Manilal was born in 1892, Ramadas in 1897, and Devadas in 1900.

Kasturbai was a great supporter of her husband and his cause. She was imprisoned several times for participating in protests. Kasturbai died in 1944 while under arrest. The couple had been married for 62 years.

▶ **When Gandhi first went to South Africa, Kasturbai and the boys stayed behind. They joined him three years later.**

Overcoming Obstacles

During the 1919 hartal, some of Gandhi's followers used violence. The British did not like the strike and reacted to the violence. This led to the deaths of more than 350 unarmed Indian people. The Amritsar Massacre caused Gandhi to despair.

Beginning in 1920, Gandhi began a boycott of anything from Great Britain. This included all British goods. In 1922, the government sentenced Gandhi to six years in jail for **disobedience** and defying British rule. He served two years in jail, but it did not deter him from his fight.

▲ Gandhi often spun cloth to make his own clothing. He encouraged his followers to do the same so they would not have to buy clothing from English clothing manufacturers.

▲ The march of followers that Gandhi led to the sea from March to April 1930 became known as the Salt March. The trek to the Arabian Sea was approximately 240 miles (386 kilometers).

The British government supplied India with its salt. The government put a very high tax on the salt and would not allow Indians to produce their own. This meant that many Indians could not afford to buy salt. Gandhi tried to change this tax. The government would not negotiate with him.

On March 12, 1930, Gandhi led a group of people on a march to the sea to challenge the tax. When they reached the sea 24 days later, Gandhi picked up a handful of sea salt. This was against the law. Indians were not allowed to possess salt not purchased from the government. Thousands of Indians began to collect salt from the beach, deliberately breaking the law. More than 60,000 Indians were arrested. Gandhi was put in jail once again.

Achievements and Successes

Eventually, the government accepted the power of Gandhi's non-violent movement. It began **negotiating** changes to the laws. Gandhi helped reach several settlements with the British government. These changes helped improve conditions for women and the poor. After a long struggle, India gained independence from Great Britain on August 15, 1947. The British government created two separate countries, dividing the region based on religion. India was primarily Hindu, and Pakistan was created for Muslims. This upset Gandhi, who believed that all religions should accept others' beliefs and live side by side with them as equals. He began a **fast** to remind the people to love, not hate.

On January 30, 1948, Gandhi was assassinated by a **radical** Hindu, Nathuram Godse. Gandhi's death was mourned around the world. In India, approximately one million people followed Gandhi's funeral procession through the streets of Delhi.

◀ **It took five hours for the procession of mourners to reach the Jumna River, where Gandhi's body was cremated.**

During his lifetime, Gandhi was considered a controversial figure. Many people in India loved and respected him. There were also many who did not agree with his beliefs. Gandhi was nominated for the Nobel Peace Prize five times. However, he never won the award. Over time, Gandhi has become an important figure of tolerance and non-violence. Many other activists have been inspired by Gandhi and his ability to stand up to injustice through peaceful means.

HELPING OTHERS

Gandhi dedicated his life to helping others. As a lawyer, he worked for free to represent the poor. He also worked to heal the sick and wounded. When a plague struck in India, Gandhi helped at the hospital for two hours every day. He also dressed the wounds of **lepers**. During his life, Gandhi set up several ashrams. These spiritual retreats were based on the principles of working and living together as equals.

▲ Gandhi set up his first ashram in India in Ahmedabad. He lived there from 1917 until 1930.

Write a Biography

A person's life story can be the subject of a book. This kind of book is called a biography. Biographies describe the lives of remarkable people, such as those who have achieved great success or have done important things to help others. These people may be alive today, or they may have lived many years ago. Reading a biography can help you learn more about a remarkable person.

At school, you might be asked to write a biography. First, decide who you want to write about. You can choose a civil rights activist, such as Mohandas Gandhi, or any other person. Then, find out if your library has any books about this person. Learn as much as you can about him or her. Write down the key events in this person's life. What was this person's childhood like? What has he or she accomplished? What are his or her goals? What makes this person special or unusual?

A concept web is a useful research tool. Read the questions in the following concept web. Answer the questions in your notebook. Your answers will help you write a biography.

Your Opinion

- What did you learn from the books you read in your research?
- Would you suggest these books to others?
- Was anything missing from these books?

Childhood

- Where and when was this person born?
- Describe his or her parents, siblings, and friends.
- Did this person grow up in unusual circumstances?

Adulthood

- Where does this individual currently reside?
- Does he or she have a family?

Writing a Biography

Main Accomplishments

- What is this person's life's work?
- Has he or she received awards or recognition for accomplishments?
- How have this person's accomplishments served others?

Work and Preparation

- What was this person's education?
- What was his or her work experience?
- How does this person work; what is or was the process he or she uses or used?

Help and Obstacles

- Did this individual have a positive attitude?
- Did he or she receive help from others?
- Did this person have a mentor?
- Did this person face any hardships?
- If so, how were the hardships overcome?

Timeline

YEAR	MOHANDAS GANDHI	WORLD EVENTS
1869	Mohandas Karamchand Gandhi is born on October 2.	The first African American labor union is created in the United States.
1882	Gandhi marries Kasturbai Makanji at age 13.	The University of Punjab opens in modern-day Pakistan.
1913	Gandhi leads the Transvaal March in South Africa and is arrested.	The British House of Commons rejects women's right to vote.
1915	Gandhi returns to India.	In New York City, 25,000 women march along Fifth Avenue, demanding the right to vote.
1930	Gandhi leads a march in protest of British control and taxation of salt.	In South Africa, white women are given the right to vote.
1947	India wins independence from British rule.	Jackie Robinson is the first African American to play in Major League Baseball.
1948	Gandhi is assassinated on January 30.	Sri Lanka and Burma declare independence from Great Britain.

Key Words

apartheid: a system where white people had more rights than other races

ashram: a building where a religious community and its leader live

authorities: the people in control; the people who have the power to control others

boycotts: refusing to use, buy, or participate in something as a way of protesting unfairness

Christianity: the religion based on the teachings of Jesus Christ

disobedience: refusal to obey the laws or rules

equality: the state of being valued the same as others

fast: choosing not to eat

Hindu: the dominant religion of India

Islam: a religion that teaches that there is only one God and that Muhammed is God's prophet

Jainism: a religion of India that believes that the soul lives forever

lepers: people suffering from leprosy, a disease that affects skin and nerves and may cause deformity

negotiating: discussing a problem in order to find a solution

non-violent: peaceful

prejudice: an unfair feeling of dislike for a particular group because of race, religion, gender, etc.

radical: someone or something that departs from tradition

segregation: keeping people of different races separate from one another

Index

Log on to www.av2books.com

AV² by Weigl brings you media enhanced books that support active learning. Go to www.av2books.com, and enter the special code found on page 2 of this book. You will gain access to enriched and enhanced content that supplements and complements this book. Content includes video, audio, weblinks, quizzes, a slide show, and activities.

AV² Online Navigation

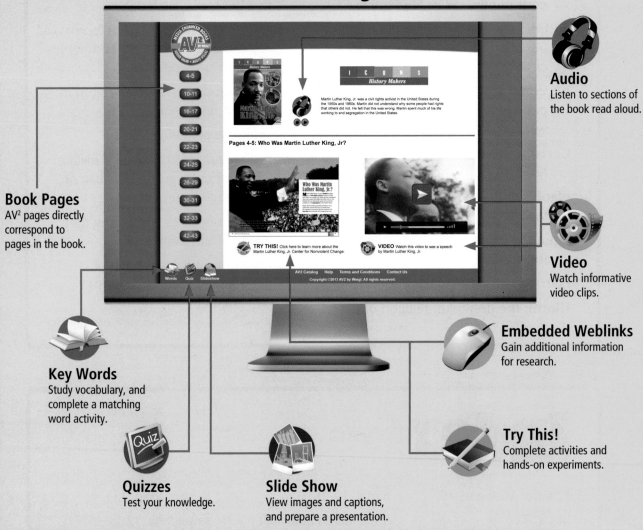

Book Pages
AV² pages directly correspond to pages in the book.

Key Words
Study vocabulary, and complete a matching word activity.

Quizzes
Test your knowledge.

Slide Show
View images and captions, and prepare a presentation.

Audio
Listen to sections of the book read aloud.

Video
Watch informative video clips.

Embedded Weblinks
Gain additional information for research.

Try This!
Complete activities and hands-on experiments.

AV² was built to bridge the gap between print and digital. We encourage you to tell us what you like and what you want to see in the future.

Sign up to be an AV² Ambassador at www.av2books.com/ambassador.